Snap books®

Gardening Guides

Enchanted Gardening

GROWING MINIATURE GARDENS, FAIRY GARDENS, AND MORE

by Lisa J. Amstutz

CAPSTONE PRESS
a capstone imprint

Snap Books are published by Capstone Press,
1710 Roe Crest Drive, North Mankato, Minnesota 56003
www.mycapstone.com

Library of Congress Cataloging-in-Publication Data
Names: Amstutz, Lisa J., author.
Title: Enchanted gardening : growing miniature gardens, fairy gardens, and
   more / by Lisa Amstutz.
Description: North Mankato, Minnesota : Capstone Press, [2016] | Series: Snap
   books. Gardening guides | Audience: Ages 8-14._ | Audience: Grades 4 to
   6._ | Includes bibliographical references.
Identifiers: LCCN 2015031202|
ISBN 9781491482346 (library binding) |
ISBN 9781491486245 (eBook PDF)
Subjects: LCSH: Gardening for children—Juvenile literature. | Gardening to
   attract wildlife—Juvenile literature. | Gardens, Miniature—Juvenile
   literature. | Container gardening—Juvenile literature.
Classification: LCC SB457 .A474 2016 | DDC 635.9—dc23
LC record available at http://lccn.loc.gov/2015031202

Editorial Credits
Abby Colich, editor; Bobbie Nuytten and Tracy McCabe, designers;
Morgan Walters and Tracy Cummins, media researchers;
Laura Manthe, production specialist

Image Credits
All photographs by Capstone Studio: Karon Dubke with the exception of:
Shutterstock: Andrey_Kuzmin (soil), Antonova Anna, Back Cover, Daria
Minaeva, 30-31, DK.samco, 8 (box), kojihirano, 16 Middle, Melica, 11,
MongPro, 16 Bottom Right, Photology1971, Front Cover (Frame), sabza, 17,
SnelsonStock, 16 Bottom Left, Tamara Kulikova, 5, 16 Top
Design Elements by Shutterstock

Printed in Canada.
102015   009223FRS16

Table of Contents

The Basics

Create your own tiny world in a fanciful fairy garden. Plant treats for the butterflies in your neighborhood. Or decorate your porch with funny flowerpot people. The projects in this book can be just the beginning of your enchanted garden artistry. Let your imagination run wild, and watch your gardening skills blossom!

Before you get started, be sure you know what your garden needs and how to take care of it.

Sunlight

Think about where you will put your garden. Some plants need lots of sunlight. Others prefer shade. For indoor plants, a south- or west-facing window is usually the best choice.

Water

Water your indoor plants several times a week. Tap water may contain chlorine or salts that can harm your plants. It is best to use rainwater or distilled water.

Depending on your climate, you may have to water your outdoor plants as well. Most need about an inch of water per week. If it doesn't rain much, give them a good soak with a hose or watering can two or three times a week.

Supplies

You'll also need a few tools and supplies. For indoor projects, you'll need a trowel, watering can or spray bottle, and potting soil. For outdoor projects, you may need a rake or hoe for getting the soil ready. You'll also want a trowel for planting and a watering can or hose. These can be found at a nursery, department store, or hardware store.

It's time to dig in. Pick up your trowel, and get ready to create little worlds with a lot of magical appeal!

Fairy Gardens Galore

What fairy wouldn't love
a little home of her own?
You can create fairy gardens
anywhere. If you only have room
indoors, try making this fairy garden.
Line a basket with moss and a few
small plants. Then add enchanted
garden decorations.

What You'll Need

- basket, about 12 inches (30 centimeters) wide
- piece of plastic or foil to line the basket
- small gravel
- potting soil
- garden moss
- small succulents or other plants discussed in the box on page 7
- miniature items such as a tire, ladder, fence, and kite (Purchase these at a craft store.)
- natural items and small household items (See the list on page 7.)

Instructions

1. Line the basket with plastic.

2. Place a layer of gravel in the bottom of the basket.

3. Fill basket with potting soil to 1 inch (2.5 cm) below the rim.

4. Arrange your plants on top of the soil. Then dig a hole with your fingers a little bigger than each plant's roots. Set the plant in the hole, and fill in soil around it. Press firmly to hold it in place.

5. Cover the remaining soil with moss. Using the items you have chosen, arrange a scene in your garden.

6. Set your garden indoors near a window or outdoors in a partially shaded spot. Mist your garden with a spray bottle whenever the soil feels dry.

PLANT CHOICES

Succulents and miniature plants work best in fairy gardens. You can use any small plants that look suitably fairy-like. Some examples include purple quail, elfin thyme, jade plants, violets, leptinella, miniature juniper, and mosaic plants.

ENDLESS POSSIBILITIES

What kind of scene do you want to build in your fairy garden? Look around your home or yard for small items to decorate your fairy garden. Set bottle caps upside down to make stepping stones. Use a spool as a fairy-sized table. Turn an acorn into a little birdhouse. Glue a marble to a golf tee to form a gazing ball. Set a shell upside down and fill with water for a birdbath. Look at the list below. What else could you make?

- *buttons*
- *washers*
- *golf tees*
- *marbles*
- *baby food jars*

- *spools*
- *bottle caps*
- *shells*
- *tiny flowers*
- *leaves*

- *stones*
- *pebbles*
- *acorns*
- *milkweed fluff*
- *pine cones*

7

Outdoor Fairy Garden

For this outdoor fairy garden, choose a shady spot near the base of a tree or in a flower bed. You can also make a fairy garden in a pot and set it outside. If you'd like, add a fairy figurine or two to your garden.

What You'll Need

- trowel
- cardboard half-gallon milk or juice carton
- small twigs, pine branches, strips of bark, or other outdoor items for outside of fairy house
- craft glue
- miniature fern plants
- garden moss
- white gravel
- small natural or household items to decorate (See the list on page 7 for ideas.)

Instructions

Plant your fairy garden in spring, once danger of frost has passed.

1. Build a small house using the instructions below. Set it in your garden.

2. With a trowel, dig a hole a little larger than the root ball of each plant. Set the plant in the hole, and fill in soil around it. Press soil firmly to hold the plant in place.

3. Lay moss over the area, and press it down gently. Water it well.

4. Make a path to the front door of the house with white gravel.

5. Arrange other items to decorate your garden. Use your imagination. What else can you add to make your garden fairy-friendly?

6. Water your plants daily for the first week. Then water two to three times per week or whenever the soil feels dry.

Fairy House Instructions

1. Cut off the lower half of the milk or juice carton, and discard it.

2. Cut an opening in one side of the carton for a door.

3. Gather small twigs, tree bark, or other natural items, and cut or break them to the height of the walls. Glue them all the way around the four sides of the house. Be sure not to cover the door.

4. Gather pine branches or other natural items, and glue them to the top of the carton as the roof. Overlap them as needed to cover the whole surface.

5. Press the fairy house into the dirt about 0.5 inch (1.3 cm) to help keep it from blowing away.

Day at the Beach

Even fairies need a vacation sometimes. Plant them their own relaxing beach garden.

What You'll Need

- large plastic or metal sand pail or container
- drill
- gravel
- potting soil
- sand
- blue glass pebbles or aquarium gravel
- small rectangle of terry cloth, 2 x 3 inches (5 x 7.5 cm) (Use part of an old towel if you have one.)
- zebra grass and jade plants

Instructions

1. Have an adult drill three holes for drainage in the bottom of the pail.

2. Place a layer of gravel in the bottom of the pail.

3. Add potting soil to 3 inches (7.5 cm) below the rim of the pail.

4. Set plants in place, and fill in potting soil around them to 1 inch (2.5 cm) below the rim. Press soil to hold the plants firmly in place.

5. Add a thin layer of sand to cover the soil. Add blue pebbles or gravel on one edge to represent water.

6. Lay out the terry cloth for a beach towel. Decorate with other small toys or natural objects.

7. Use a spray bottle to mist your garden two to three times per week or as needed to keep the soil moist.

ADD PROPS 🌿

Add a mini drink umbrella to provide your fairy with some shade.

MORE PLANT CHOICES 🌿

Other plants to try in your beach garden are jade "princess pine," parlor palm, mini rush (toe tickling grass), and silver bush plants.

Flower Fairies

Plant a row of hollyhocks to make elegant fairies. Children have been making these traditional flower dolls for hundreds of years. You can make fairies with other kinds of flowers as well.

What You'll Need

- 6 hollyhock plants
- bamboo stakes
- twine
- toothpick

Instructions

Plant hollyhocks in spring or fall. Choose a sunny spot that is sheltered from the wind.

1. Dig a hole for each plant large enough to set the entire root ball inside. Plants should be spaced 18 inches (46 cm) apart.

2. Remove hollyhock plants from their pots, and set them in the holes. Fill in with soil around them. Press soil firmly to hold them in place.

3. Water your new plants daily for the first week. Then water once or twice a week if the weather is hot and dry. If you live in a very dry climate, you may need to water them more often.

4. When the plants grow tall, push a bamboo stake into the ground beside each one. Gently tie the stem to the stake with twine.

5. Harvest the flowers after they fully open. Remove any seed heads that form on the plants. Chop them off at the base once the flowers finish blooming. In some areas the plants will regrow for several years.

Flower Fairy Instructions

1. Pick several fresh hollyhock flowers and one flower bud. Remove the stamens and pistils from the center of the flowers.

2. Slide toothpick through the center of one flower. The upside-down flower will serve as the fairy's dress. Add additional flowers to form layers.

3. Stick a flower bud on top of the toothpick for a head.

4. Add an upside-down flower hat.

Butterfly Bistro

Plant these colorful flowers and in a few months, your butterfly bistro will be open for business. Butterflies love to sip the sweet nectar.

What You'll Need

- 3 flowerpots, 12 inches (30 cm) in diameter
- 1 terra-cotta flowerpot with a saucer, 6 inches (15 cm) in diameter
- potting soil
- craft or wood glue
- several large rocks
- "graffiti lipstick" pentas, lantana, and nasturtium seeds or plants

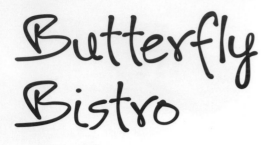

Instructions

Plant your butterfly garden on the south side of your home if possible. The spot should be sunny but sheltered from the wind. Plant seeds or plants in late spring, once danger of frost has passed.

1. If you are using plant starts, fill each large flowerpot halfway with soil. Set a plant inside. Fill in soil around the plant, and press firmly to hold it in place. If you are planting seeds, fill pot with soil to 1 inch (2.5 cm) below the rim. Sprinkle seeds on top. Cover with a thin layer of soil about 1/8 inch (3 mm) thick.

2. Set small flowerpot upside down. Glue saucer on top of the upside-down pot. Let glue dry.

3. Fill saucer with water, and add several large rocks for the butterflies to rest on.

4. Arrange pots and water dish in a pleasing way. Set them in a sunny spot.

5. Water plants daily. Refill dish as needed.

PRETTY POTS

Paint your pots and water dish a bright color to help attract butterflies.

BUTTERFLY FAVORITES
To help make sure butterflies will come, find out what species live in your area. Grow their favorite plants in your butterfly garden.

Hummingbird Haven

Advertise for hummingbirds by planting their favorite foods. These acrobatic little birds are fun to watch!

What You'll Need

- large flowerpot, 12 inches (30 cm) in diameter (Use a hanging container if desired.)
- potting soil
- 1 "fireball" bee balm, 2 trailing petunia, and 2 lantana plants

Instructions

Plant seeds or starts in late spring, once the danger of frost has passed.

1. Fill pot with potting soil to 3 inches (7.5 cm) below the rim. Set plants inside. Place petunias and lantana around the edge and bee balm in the center.

2. Add soil around the plants to within 1 inch (2.5 cm) of the rim. Press firmly to hold plants in place.

3. Set or hang the pot in a sunny spot. Water it daily.

ADD A BIRDBATH

Your hummingbirds may want a quick bath after stopping by for some nectar. If there's room in your garden, add a birdbath. If you don't have one, have an adult help you research ways to make one yourself.

MORE HUMMINGBIRD FAVORITES

Try planting any of these plants around your home to attract more hummingbirds.

- honeysuckle
- fuchsia
- cardinal flower
- trumpet vine
- yucca
- tiger lily
- blazing star
- hollyhock
- butterfly weed
- blazing star
- fairy duster
- foxglove

If you live in the southwestern United States, try these plants:

- jojoba
- chuparosa
- red yucca
- yellow columbine
- penstemon
- ocotillo
- fairy duster
- red sage
- claret cup cactus
- toyon

Moonbeam Garden

This moon-shaped garden looks magical on a moonlit night. The night-flowering plants seem to glow. White flowers often open at night to attract nocturnal pollinators such as moths and bats. The plants' white color makes them easy to find in the dark. They may give off a strong fragrance as well.

What You'll Need

- crescent-shaped garden bed, 2 feet (61 cm) long (See sidebar for instructions. If you don't have space for a garden bed, use a planter and set it outside.)
- trowel
- white gravel
- any combination of the following plants: dusty miller, lamb's ear, night phlox, silver artemisia, white yarrow, yucca, candytuft, Shasta daisy, or white delphinium

Instructions

1. Prepare garden bed. Set larger plants in the center and border plants around the edges of the bed.
2. With your trowel, dig a hole a little larger than each plant's roots.
3. Set the plant in the hole, and fill in around it with soil. Press firmly to hold the plant in place.
4. Spread white gravel around the plants for an extra moonlit glow.
5. Water your new plants daily for the first week. Then water once or twice a week if the weather is dry.

ADD MORE GLOW

String small white lights around your garden or set out battery-operated tea lights in mason jars for an extra glow.

HOW TO PREPARE A GARDEN BED

Get the ground ready if you're planting outside. If you're starting a new garden, remove any grass and weeds with a spade. Turn and mix up the soil well. If you have very sandy or heavy clay soil, mix in some compost, manure, or peat moss. Rake out any clumps of weeds and large stones. Then smooth out the soil. If you've already used the area for a garden, remove any weeds. Loosen the soil before smoothing it out.

Happy Critter Garden

Have a "ball" with this fanciful garden! Paint happy little golf ball critters. Then plant them a cozy garden home.

What You'll Need

- 🍃 4 white golf balls
- 🍃 green, orange, black, white, yellow, dark green, and light green acrylic craft paints
- 🍃 small craft paintbrush
- 🍃 shallow pot or tray
- 🍃 potting soil
- 🍃 small aluminum plant and artillery fern (If you can't find these, try another small houseplant such as a spider plant, aloe, coleus, or sedum.)
- 🍃 moss

Instructions

1. Following the directions below, paint golf balls and let dry overnight.

For beetles:

Paint one ball dark green and one orange. Let the paint dry. On each golf ball, paint a black circle for a head, a line down the back, antennae, and several spots. Let the paint dry thoroughly. Paint two white spots for eyes. Let dry. Add pupils with black paint. Let dry overnight.

For bumblebee:

Paint one ball yellow and let it dry. Paint a black circle for the head, and black stripes. Let dry. Paint two white spots for eyes. Let dry. Paint pupils with black paint. Let dry overnight.

For frog:

Paint ball black, and let it dry. Paint a light green face and chest. Let dry. Paint two white spots for eyes. With black paint, add pupils to the eyes, and paint mouth, nostrils, spots, and outline of legs.

2. Fill container half-full of soil. Set aluminum plant and artillery fern on top. Fill in soil around the plants, and press firmly to hold them in place. Leave 0.5 inch (1.3 cm) of space at the top

3. Cover the remaining surface with moss.

4. Set frog, beetles, and bumblebee in the garden.

5. Mist your garden with a clean spray bottle as needed to keep the soil moist.

STONE CRITTERS 🌿

Try painting critters on stones instead. Look for stones shaped like the animals you want to paint.

Gorgeous Gourd Planters

This sparkling centerpiece is perfect for fall decorating!

What You'll Need

- 3 fresh gourds
- gold paint
- paintbrush
- clear glitter glue
- potting soil
- sharp knife
- ornamental grass or succulent plants

Instructions

1. Paint gourds gold. Let the paint dry well. Brush on a coat of clear glitter glue to add sparkle. Let glue dry.

2. Have an adult help you cut a hole in the top of each gourd. The hole should be large enough to hold the plant.

3. Fill each hole half full of potting soil.

4. Set plants inside the holes. Fill in with potting soil around them.

5. Water your plants well.

6. Set the planters near a sunny window. Mist with spray bottle two to three times a week, or as needed.

7. If the gourds start to rot, move the plants to a new planter or plant them outdoors.

Gnome Home

Turn a broken pot into a charming little gnome home.
A few toadstools will help your gnome feel welcome.
This is a great way to recycle a broken pot, but if you
don't have one around, you can make your own.

What You'll Need

- large terra-cotta pot, 10 to 12 inches (25 to 30 cm) in diameter, preferably broken
- Dremel tool or another power tool with a carbide cutting tip (if pot is not already broken)
- goggles
- potting soil
- garden moss
- pebbles (for a path)
- gnomes and other small decorations
- smooth stones (for toadstools)
- red and white enamel paint
- paintbrush
- golf tee
- craft glue
- 1 small asparagus fern, 3 baby's tears, and 1 mosaic plant
- garden moss

Instructions

1. If the pot is not already broken, have an adult cut out a large U shape with the Dremel or other power tool. Be sure to wear safety goggles, as a lot of dust will come off the pot as it's being cut. Soaking the pot in water first will make it softer and easier to cut. Break the cut-out piece into several smaller chunks.

2. Fill the pot with potting soil. Push the broken pieces of pot into the soil to form terraces and steps as shown.

3. Dig small holes for the plants. Set the roots inside, and press soil around them to hold them in place.

4. Place moss on top of any bare soil, and press down gently.

5. Add pebbles to form a path.

6. Paint stones red. Let paint dry. Add white spots. Let dry again. Glue each stone to the top of a golf tee to form a toadstool. Add to your gnome home.

7. Add other decorations and gnomes as desired. Set the pot in a partially shaded spot outdoors, or indoors near a window.

8. Water outdoor homes daily. Water indoor homes two to three times per week.

Cheery Chick Planter

Gardens don't get any cuter than this! Try making more planters using other pastel colors.

What You'll Need

- glass jar
- yellow, orange, and black enamel or acrylic paint
- paintbrush
- yellow cupcake liner
- scissors
- craft glue
- potting soil
- baby's tears plant

MORE PLANT CHOICES 🌿

*Instead of baby's tears, try planting grass seed,
African violet, shamrock, or hen and chicks plants
in your chick planter.*

Instructions

1. Paint the jar, and let it dry thoroughly. Add a second coat if needed, and let dry again.

2. Paint two black dots for eyes and an orange triangle for a beak. Let paint dry.

3. Fold cupcake liner in half. Cut it across the middle. Fold each half in half again and glue to the sides of the jar.

4. Fill jar with potting soil to 3 inches (7.5 cm) below the rim.

5. Set baby's tears plant inside, and fill in around it with soil. Water it well.

6. Set your planter in a sunny spot. Mist with a clean spray bottle two to three times a week or as needed.

Flowerpot Friends

Assemble one of these friendly pot people, and then add hair! Set your flowerpot friend in a garden or flower bed, or prop it in a sunny window indoors.

What You'll Need

- 2 terra-cotta pots, 6 inches (15 cm) in diameter
- 6 terra-cotta pots, 2 inches (5 cm) in diameter
- 1 terra-cotta saucer, 8 inches (20 cm) in diameter
- outdoor paint
- paintbrush
- hot glue gun with glue
- markers or paint and paintbrush to draw on face
- 2 lengths of nylon cord, 18 inches (45 cm) each (Make sure it is thin enough to fit through the holes in the small pots.)
- craft stick
- 6 metal washers
- potting soil
- grass seed, grass, or other household plants that look like hair
- buttons, fabric, or other materials to dress up your flowerpot person

Instructions

1. Set one 6-inch (15-cm) pot upside down. This will be the shirt. Paint it a solid color. Let paint dry for several hours. Add a second coat if needed. Let dry again.

2. Paint the 6 small flowerpots the same color. Let dry.

3. Set the other 6-inch (15-cm) pot right side up. This will be the head. Draw on a face with permanent marker, or paint with paint and paintbrush.

4. Tie the end of one cord around a washer. String it through the hole in a 2-inch (5-cm) pot so the washer is hidden inside. About 1.5 inches (3.8 cm) above the first pot, tie another washer. String the second pot on so the washer is inside. Repeat for the third pot.

5. Repeat step 5 for the other arm.

6. Take the leftover cord at the end of the arms and string both pieces up through the hole in the bottom of the head. Adjust the arms to where you want them to be, and tie the cords around a craft stick to hold them in place.

7. Glue the head to the body with a hot glue gun. Make sure the arms hang out to the sides.

8. Fill pot with potting soil. Sprinkle grass seed on top, or plant other plants.

9. Water plants well. Set your flowerpot friend on your patio, in a flower bed or garden, or in a sunny windowsill.

10. Water daily if the pot is outdoors. Water two to three times a week if your plant is indoors.

CHANGE IT UP 🌿

☞ Dress up your flowerpot friend with a colorful headband, necktie, or scarf.

☞ Try planting begonias, impatiens, or a fern in the top.

☞ Make a friend for your flowerpot person.

What Plants Will Grow Best?

Depending where you live, it may be difficult to grow some of the outdoor plants in this book. Perhaps your climate is hot and dry or the growing season is very short. There is no one-size-fits-all when it comes to gardening.

Does that mean you can't do these projects? Not at all. Just swap out the suggested plants for others that grow well in your area. The best way to select plants is to look at your plant hardiness zone.

A plant hardiness zone is a number based on the minimum winter temperature of an area. Plant labels usually say which zones the plant is best suited for. It may grow well in zones 4 to 9, for instance, or in zones 5 and higher.

The United States Department of Agriculture (USDA) created a map of the United States showing 12 different hardiness zones. You can find this map on the USDA website. Visit the Natural Resources Canada website for a similar Canadian map.

Read More

Brown, Renata Fossen. *Gardening Lab for Kids*. Hands-On Family. Beverly, Mass.: Quarry Books, 2014.

Kuskowski, Alex. *Super Simple Butterfly Gardens: A Kid's Guide to Gardening*. Super Simple Gardening. Minneapolis: ABDO Publishing Company, 2015.

Walsh, Liza Gardner. *Fairy Garden Handbook*. Camden, Maine: Down East, 2013.

Internet Sites

FactHound offers a safe, fun way to find Internet sites related to this book. All of the sites on FactHound have been researched by our staff.

Here's all you do:

Visit *www.facthound.com*

Type in this code: 9781491482346

Super-cool stuff! Check out projects, games and lots more at **www.capstonekids.com**

Books in this series: